slimvolume

'AAABBDDEE
FGGHHIIJJK!
KLLMNNOOP
INCOMPLE E

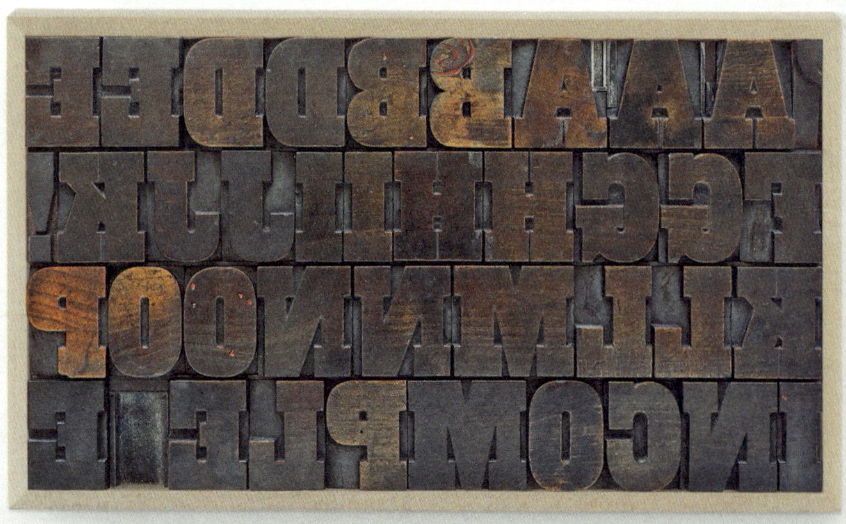

Pavel Büchler

Variable Pieces

In 1988, a small proofing press with a bed measuring 15 × 25 inches that had belonged to my friend, the painter, typographer and graphic artist, Edward Wright came into my hands. Twenty-three years on, in 2011, the newspaper designer Edwin Taylor offered me several more-or-less complete sets of wood type, alongside a number of other loose samples that had also belonged to Edward. Some time later, another friend, the artist J. H. Kocman, gave me an assortment of modern plastic letters from the Czech font Pražské Kamenné (Prague Stone Gothic) that had been discarded as surplus from an art school in Brno. The imperfections, limitations, and obsolete honesty of this equipment, with which I make most of my prints, make the works what they are.

P. B.

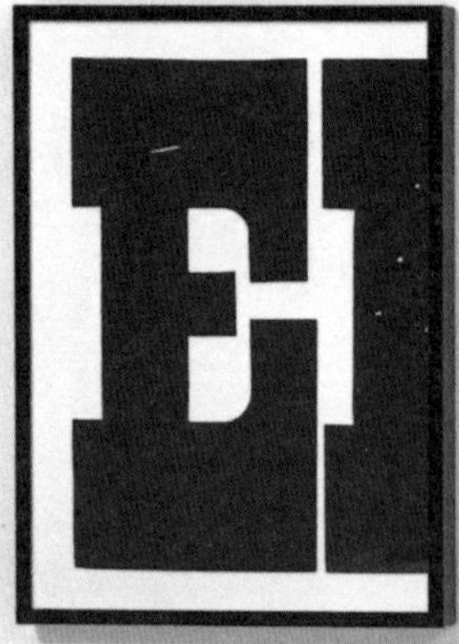

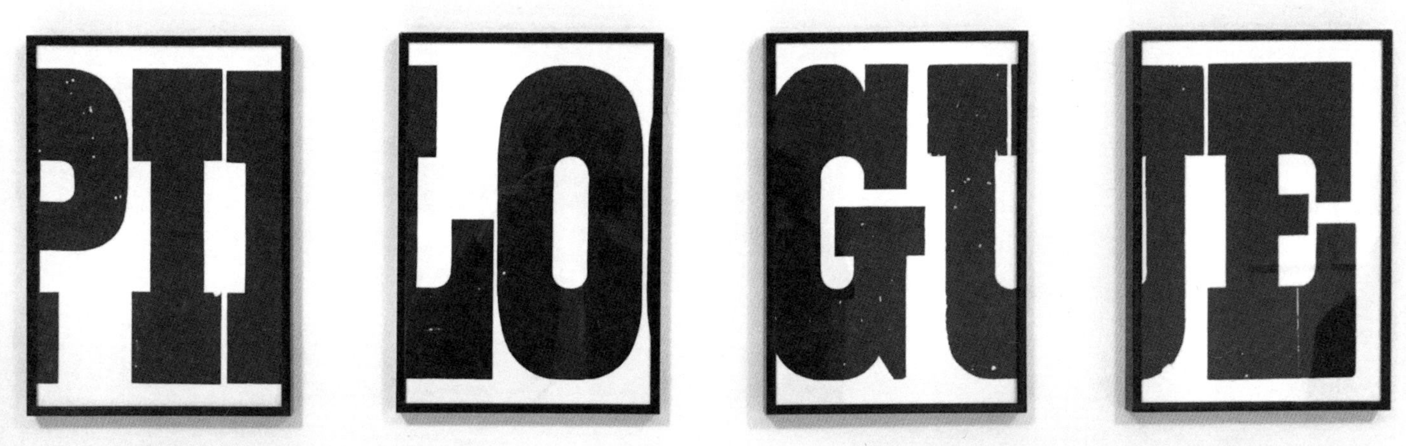PI LO GU E

HONEST WORK

BOTTOM RIGHT

WOODS AS WORDS

SIGNS OF LIFE

SPIRIT & SPIT

SO
SIMPLE
AND
DEAD

WOODWORN

WHITE AS BLACK

VIOLENT

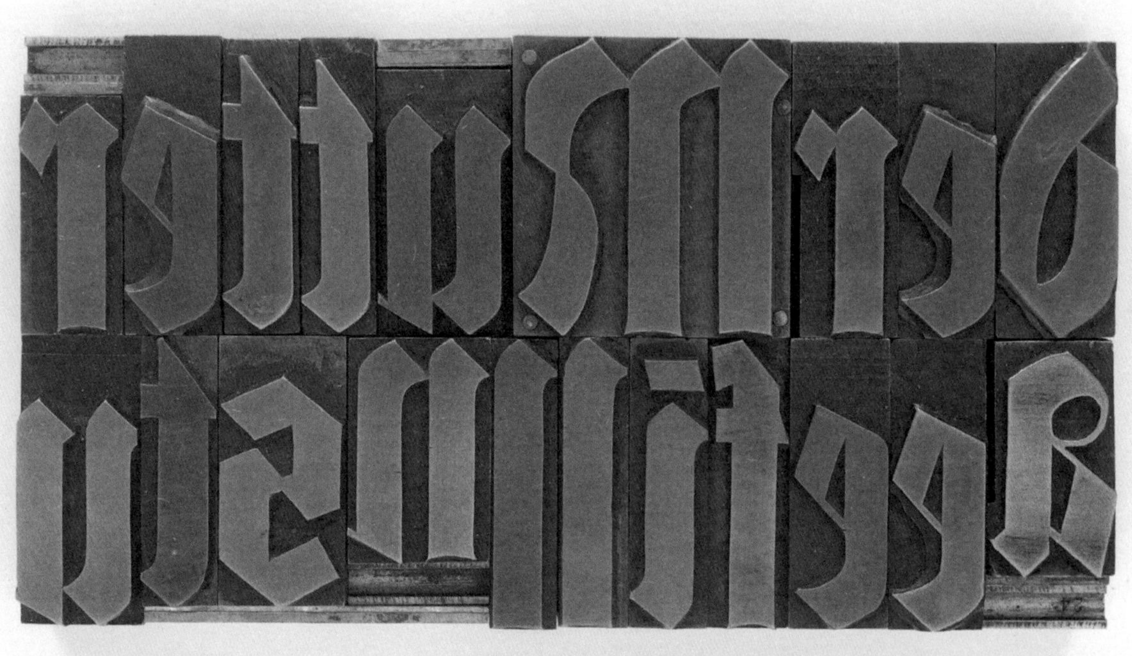

der Mutter

UNIQUE

WORD OF MOUTH

WORDS BY HAND

PAROLE ON PROBATION

POOR. OLD.

TIRED.

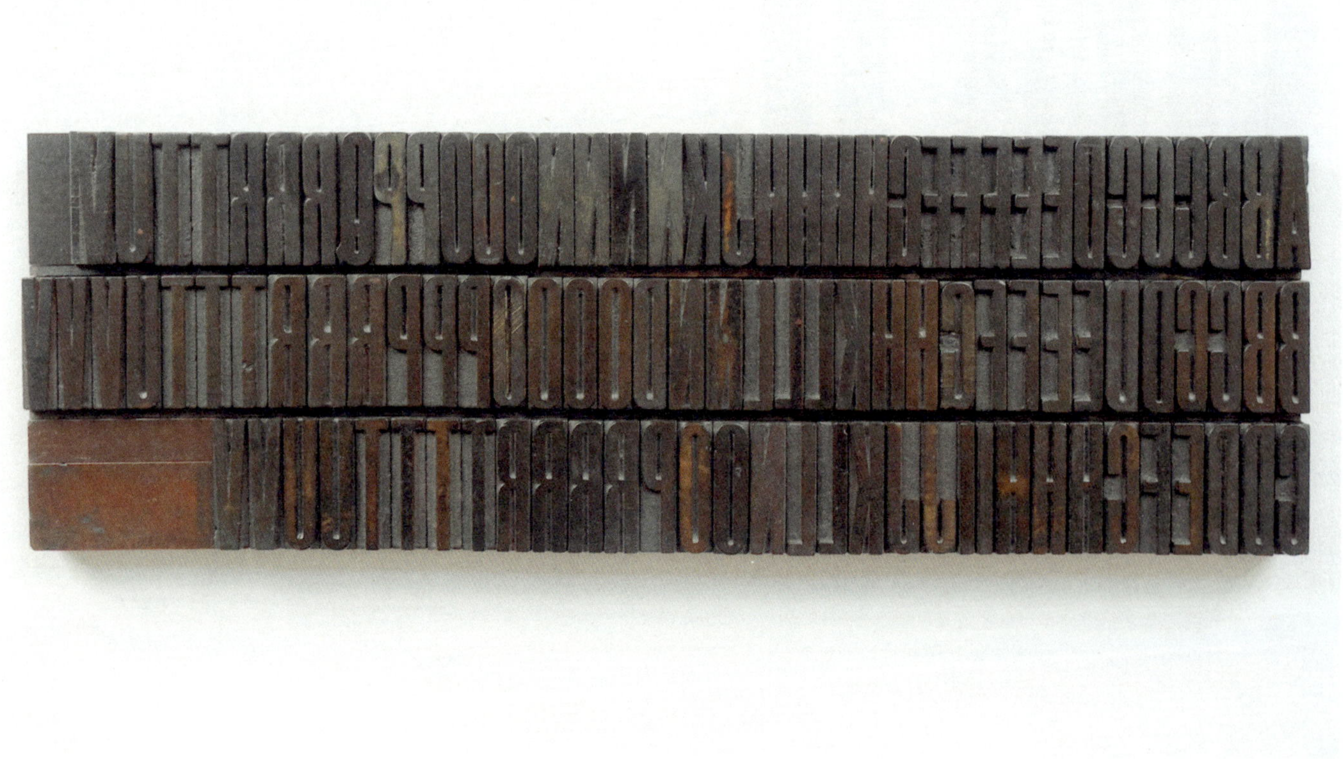

BBCCFFHHHJKNNNNPPQUV
FOR GOD THE CREATOR
BBCCDFHKLLLNPPPRTVVV
FOR GODOT THE UNDOER
CHJJKLNPRRTUUVV
FOR THE THIRD OLD GIT

ABDFGHIJKLMNOPQRSUVWXYZ ETC
ABDFGHIKLMNOPRSVUWY ETC
ADFGHILMNOPRSUY ETC
ADHILMNOPRSU ETC
AHINORS ET
AINOS ET
ET
E

ELEMMMMMENTI ESSENZIALI DDDDELLA
NNNNOSTTTTTTRRRRRA PPPPOOOOOEESSSSIIIAAA
BBCCCCFFFGGGHHHHHHJKKQUUUUVVWWXYYY

THERE, THE PHRASE EXCEEDED TH CONTNT.
 AAAAABB CC DD   FFFGGG   HIIIIIIJKKLLLL
MMMM NNNN OOOOO PPPQ RRR SSSSS   TT
UUUUVVWW YYYZ

HERE THE CONTENT EXCEEDS THE PHRAS.
 AAAAABB CC DDD   FFFGGG   HIIIIIIJKKLLLL
MMMM   NNNN OOOO PPPQ RRR SSSS   TTT
UUUUVVWW YYYZ

TWENTY FOUR OUT OF ONE H NDRED

SEVENTY SIX OUT OF NE HUNDRED
AAAAAABBCCCCEGGGHHHIIIIIJKKLLLLM
MMMPPPPQRRSSSSTTVWYZ

NO NEW WORK

R CEIVED
IDEAS
AND
MEANS

NO TIME TO PAINT

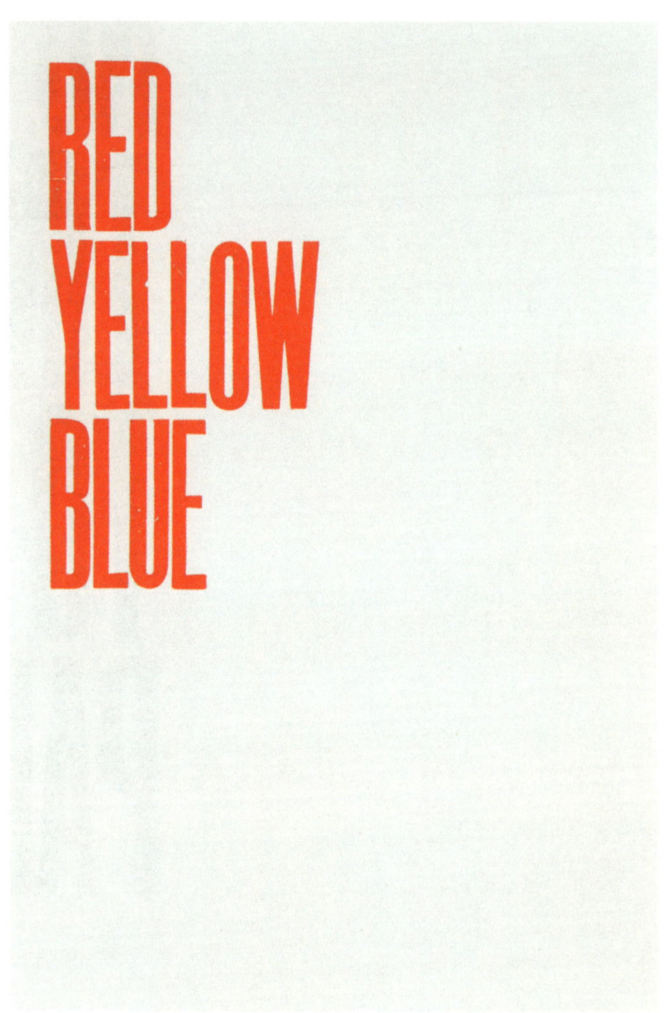
RED
YELLOW
BLUE

RED
YELLOW
BLUE

RED
YELLOW
BLUE

RED
YELLOW
BLUE

RED
YELLOW
BLUE

RED
YELLOW
BLUE

MEN AT WORK
BCD FGHIJ L
PQ S UV XYZ

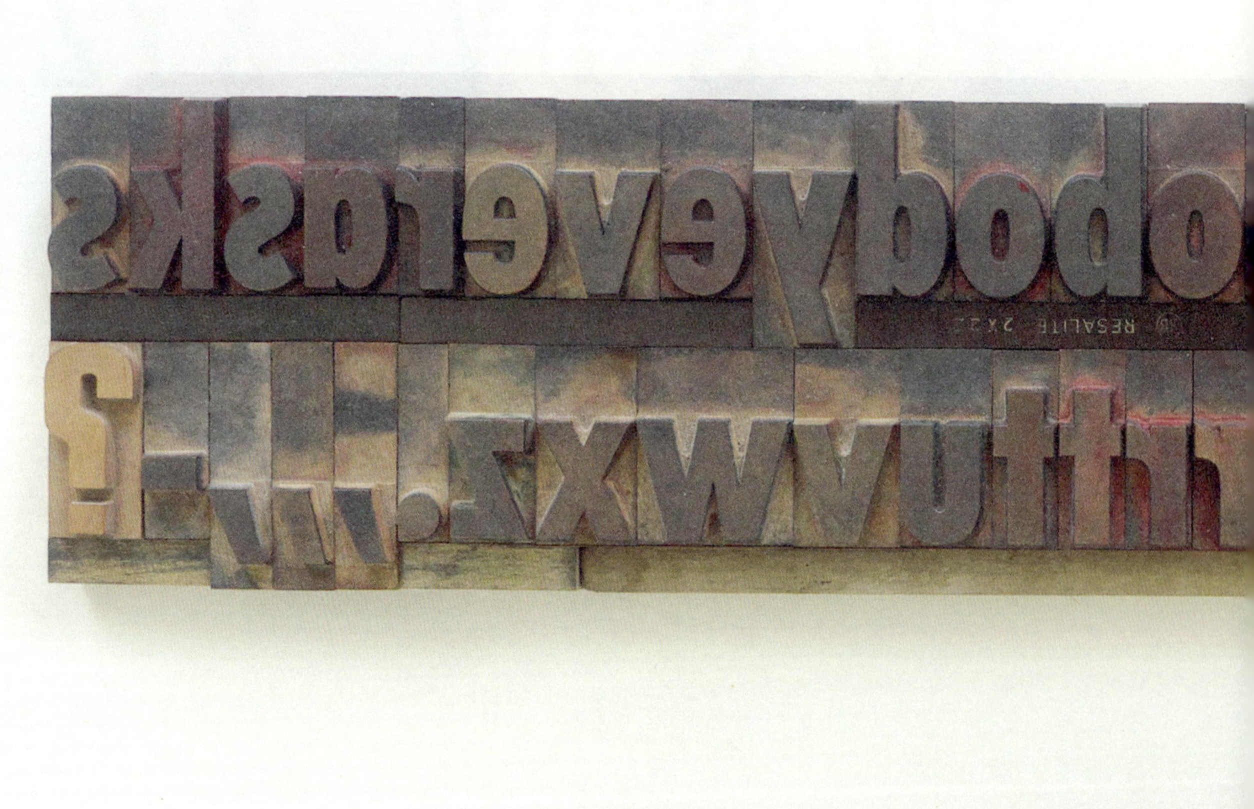

the question nobody ever asks

adehiíjklmrstuvy
hlas víry je diktum

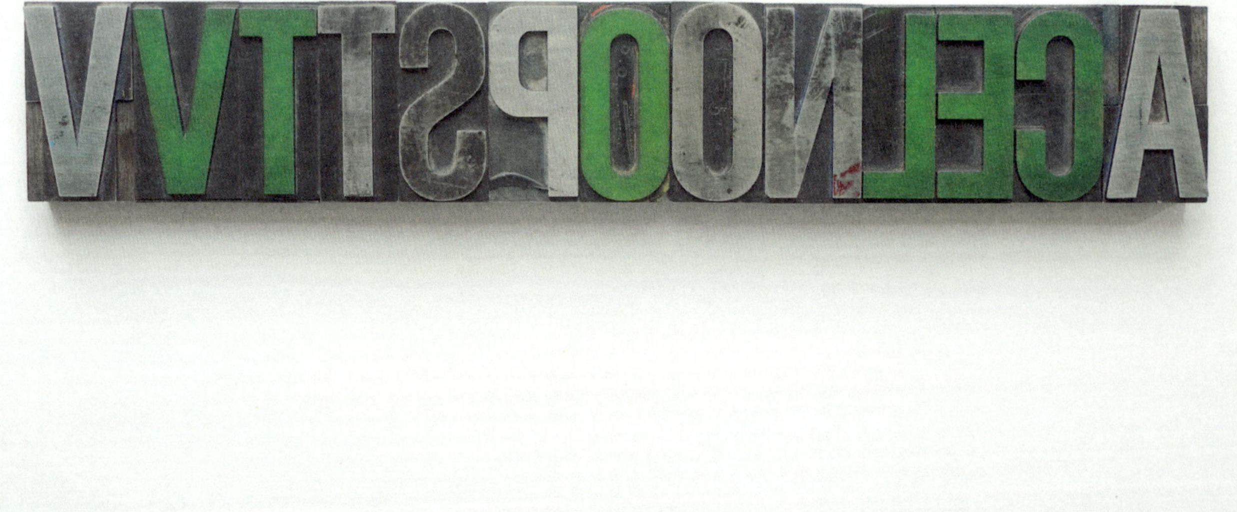

ACELNOOPSTTVV

A PAUSE,

MORE OR LESS LONG

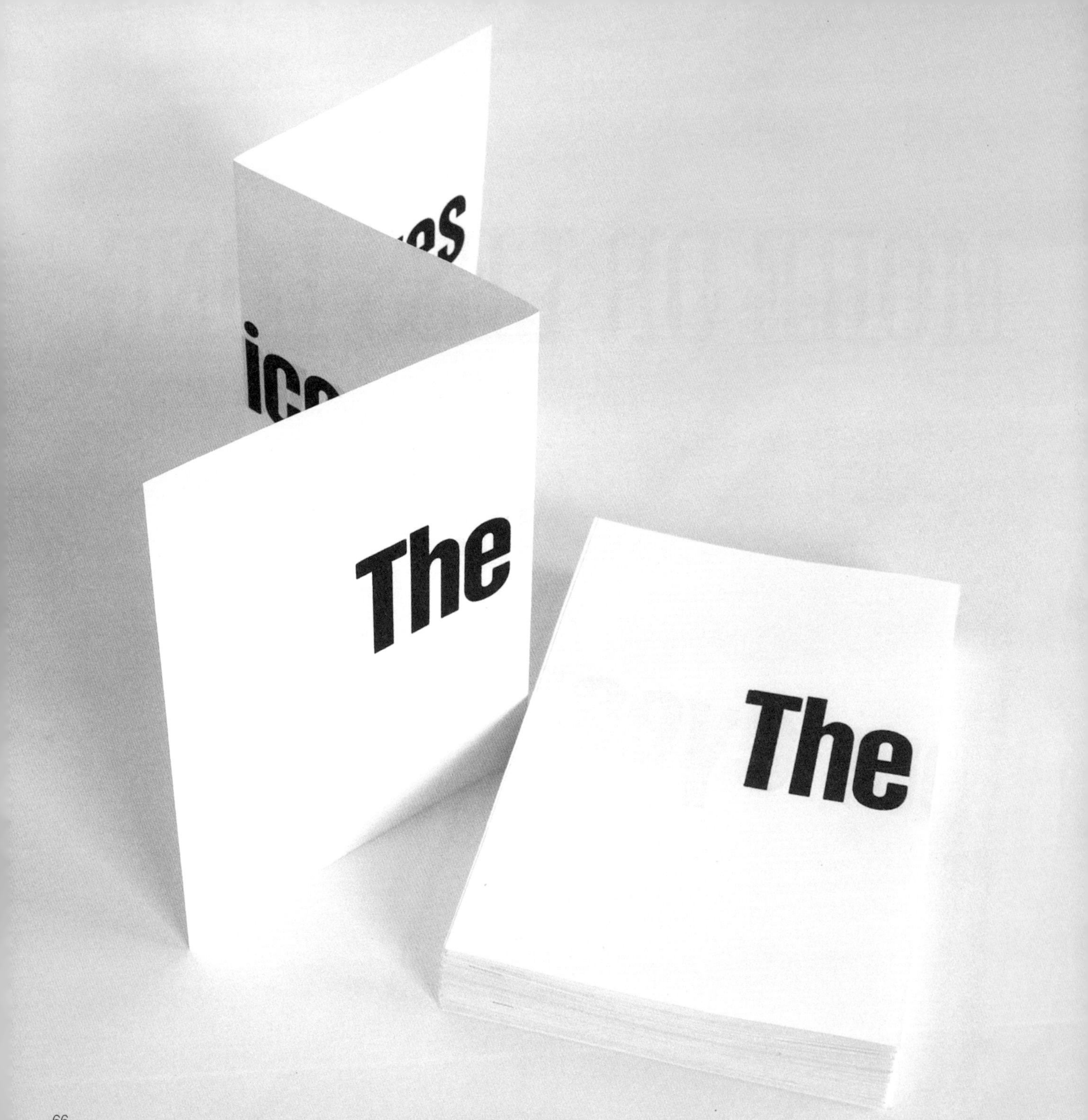

The ice in your voice the yes in your eyes

stilllife

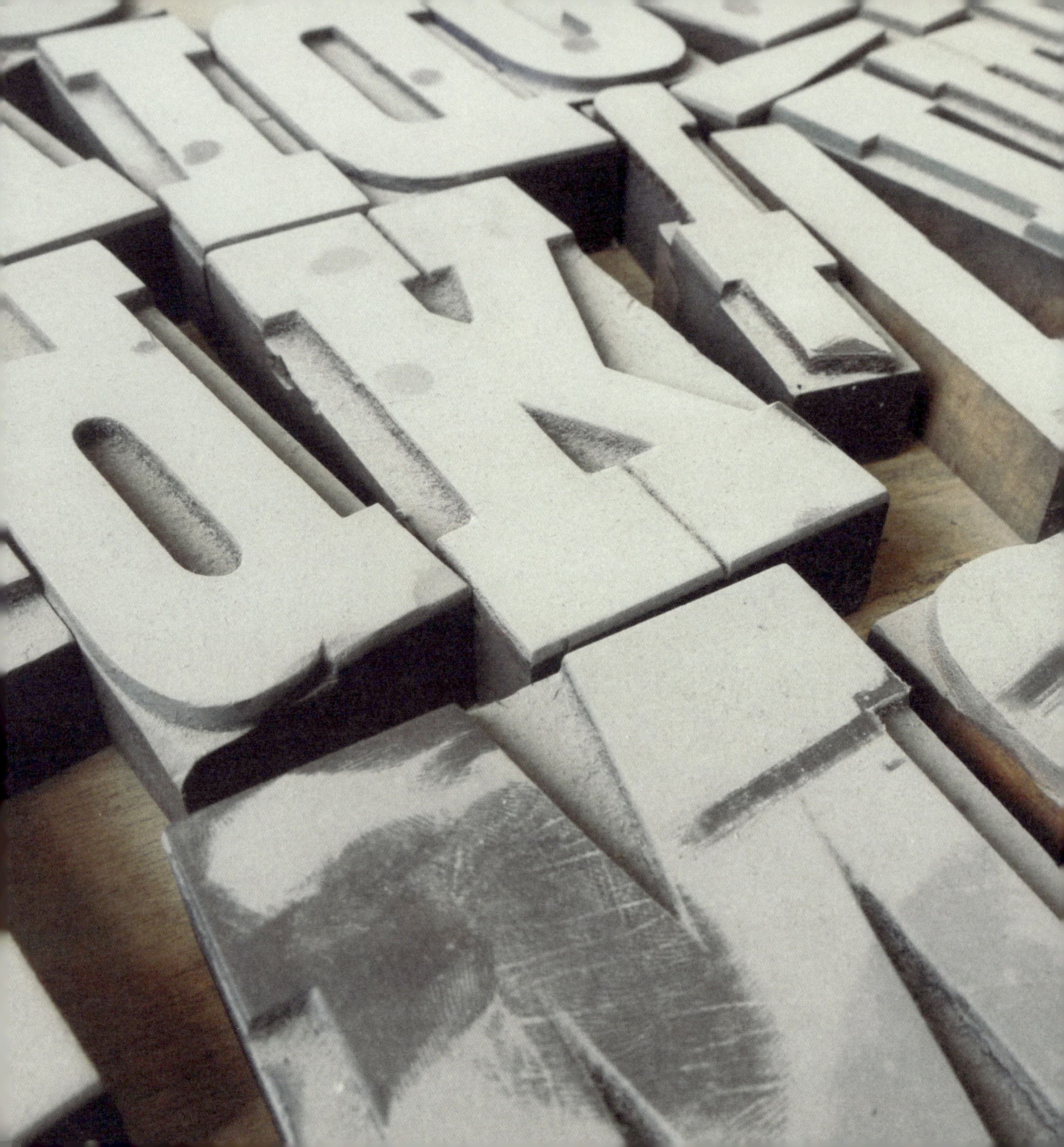

do not disturb

ONE HUNDRED AND TWENTY FOUR PIECES OF AMERICAN MAPLE IN A BOX OF IRISH OAK ABBCDDDGGGH IIJJJKKLLLLLLLLMMMOPQQRRRSSS SSTTTTTTTUUUUUVVVWWWXYYYZZ

VAINLY I HAD SOUGHT TO BORROW
FROM MY BOOKS AAAABCCCDDDD
EEEEEFFCHIIIJJJKKKLLLLLMMNPPP
QQRRRSSSSTTTTUUUUUVVWWW
XXYZZ NLY THIS AND NTHING MRE

THE MURDER MYSTERY
OF EDGAR ALLAN POE
EAIODHNRSTUYCFGLMWBKPQXZ
ABCDEFGHIJKLMNOPQRSTUVWXYZ
LE SUICIDE
DE LOUIS ARAGON

TRY
POE
FOR
POE
TRY

DON'T

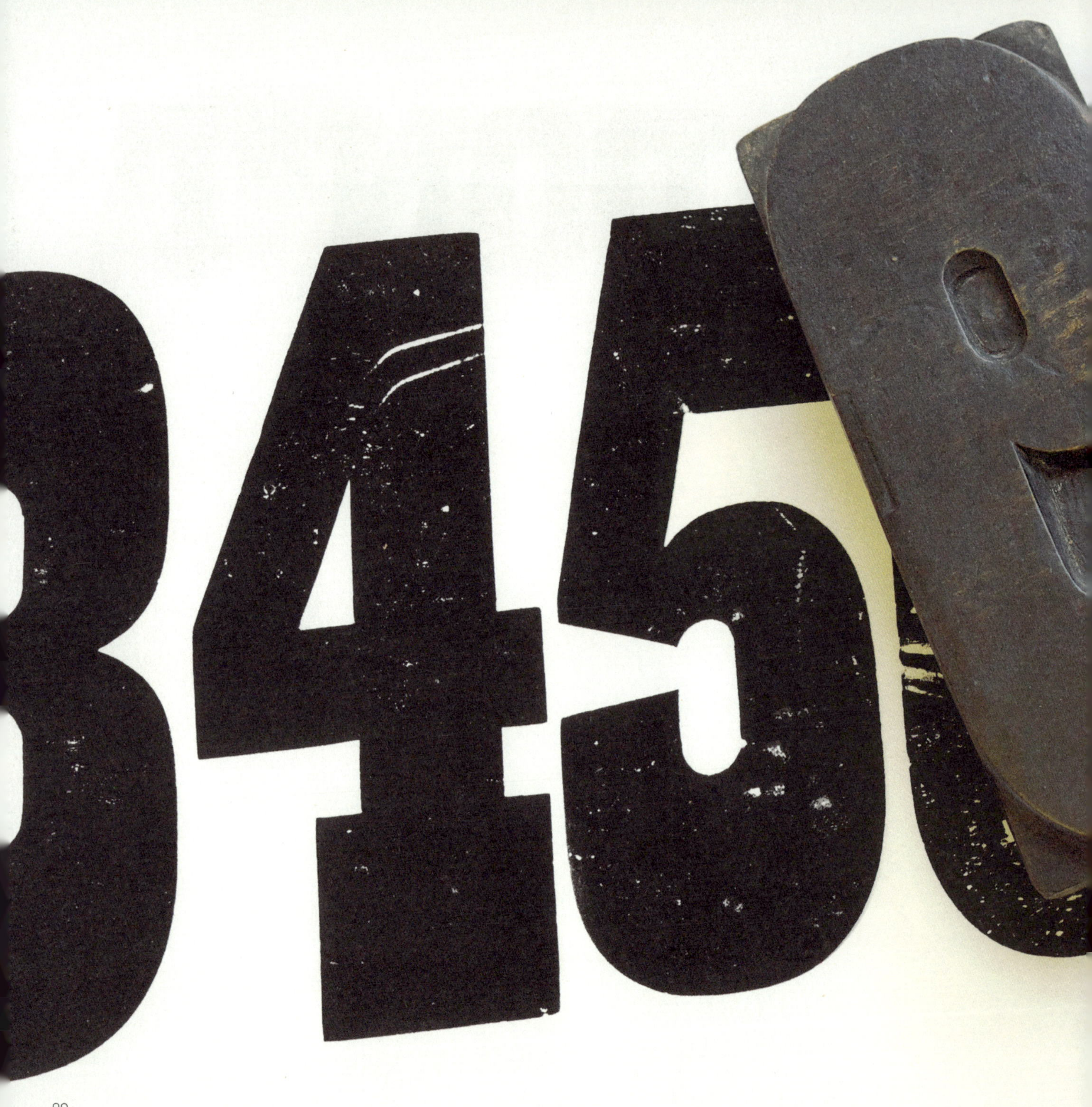

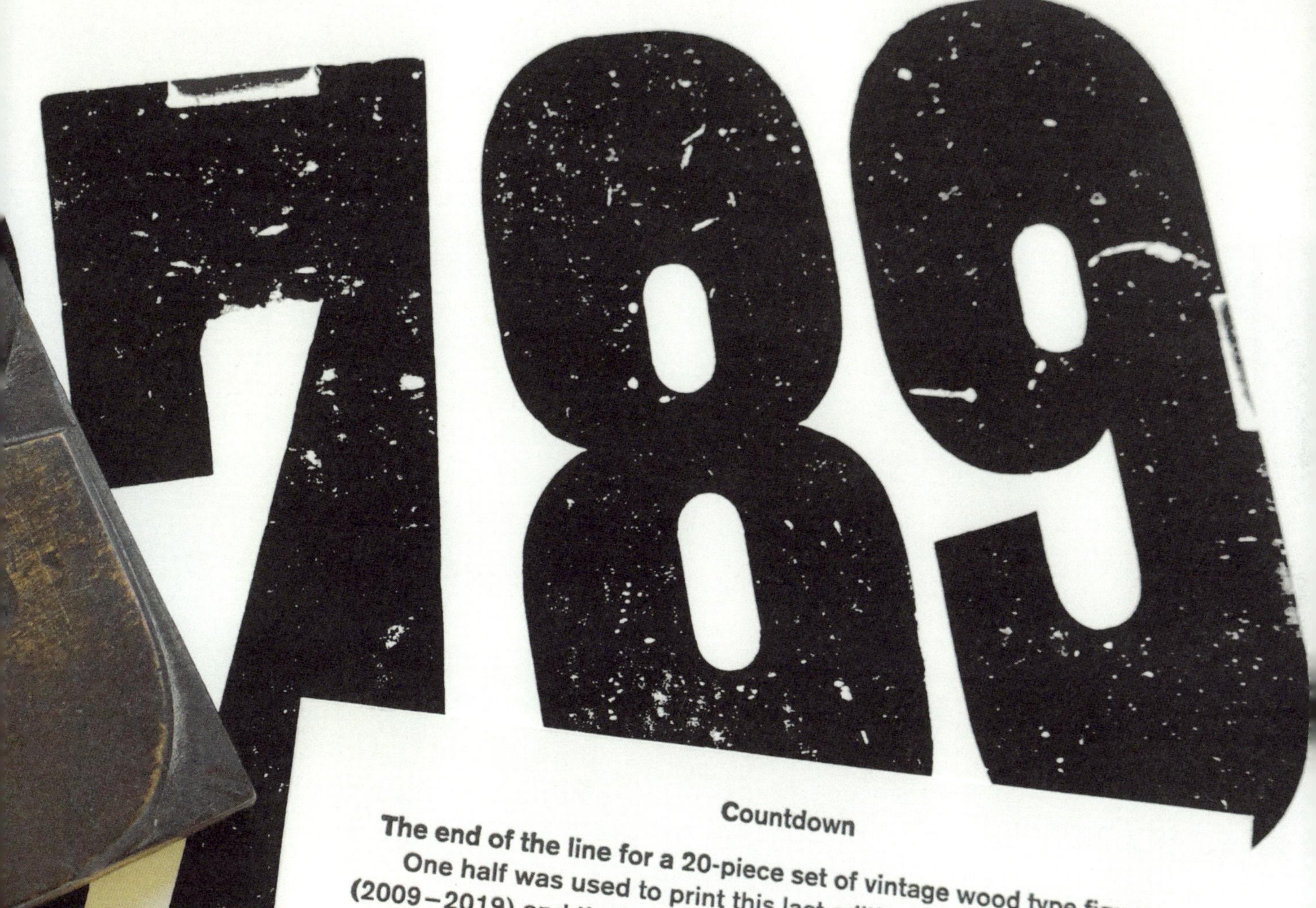

Countdown
The end of the line for a 20-piece set of vintage wood type figures. One half was used to print this last edition of MOREpublishers (2009–2019) and the other to make a parallel series of 10 prints titled While Stocks Last. The prints are distributed in the descending order (9–0), each with the wood block last used in its production.

No. 9. Pavel Büchler   November 2019

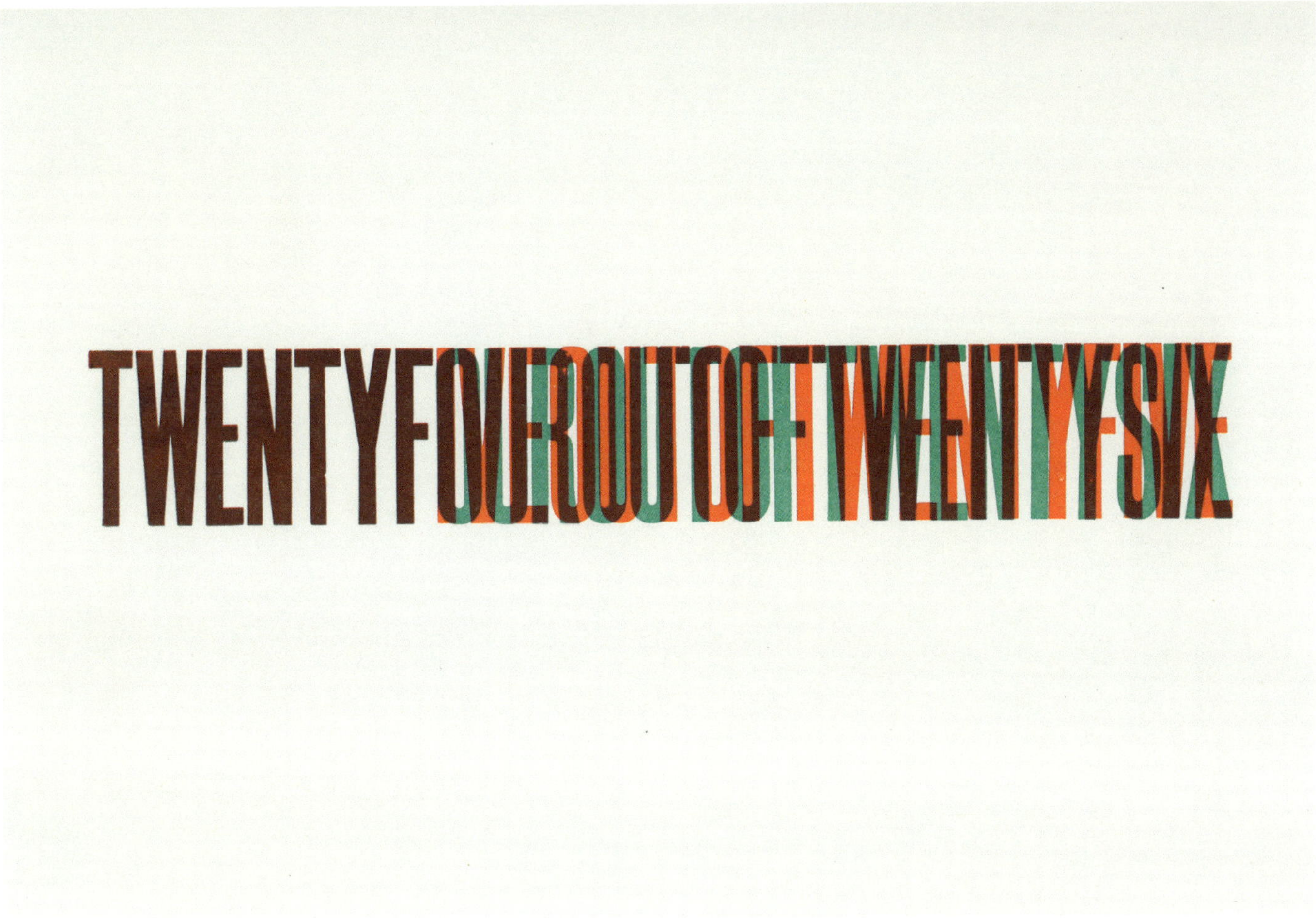

TWENTYFOUROUTOFTWENTYSIX

NINEPLUSSEVENTEEN

FIVE
WORDS
IN
A
LINE

ONE AND THREE WORDS

EINWORT

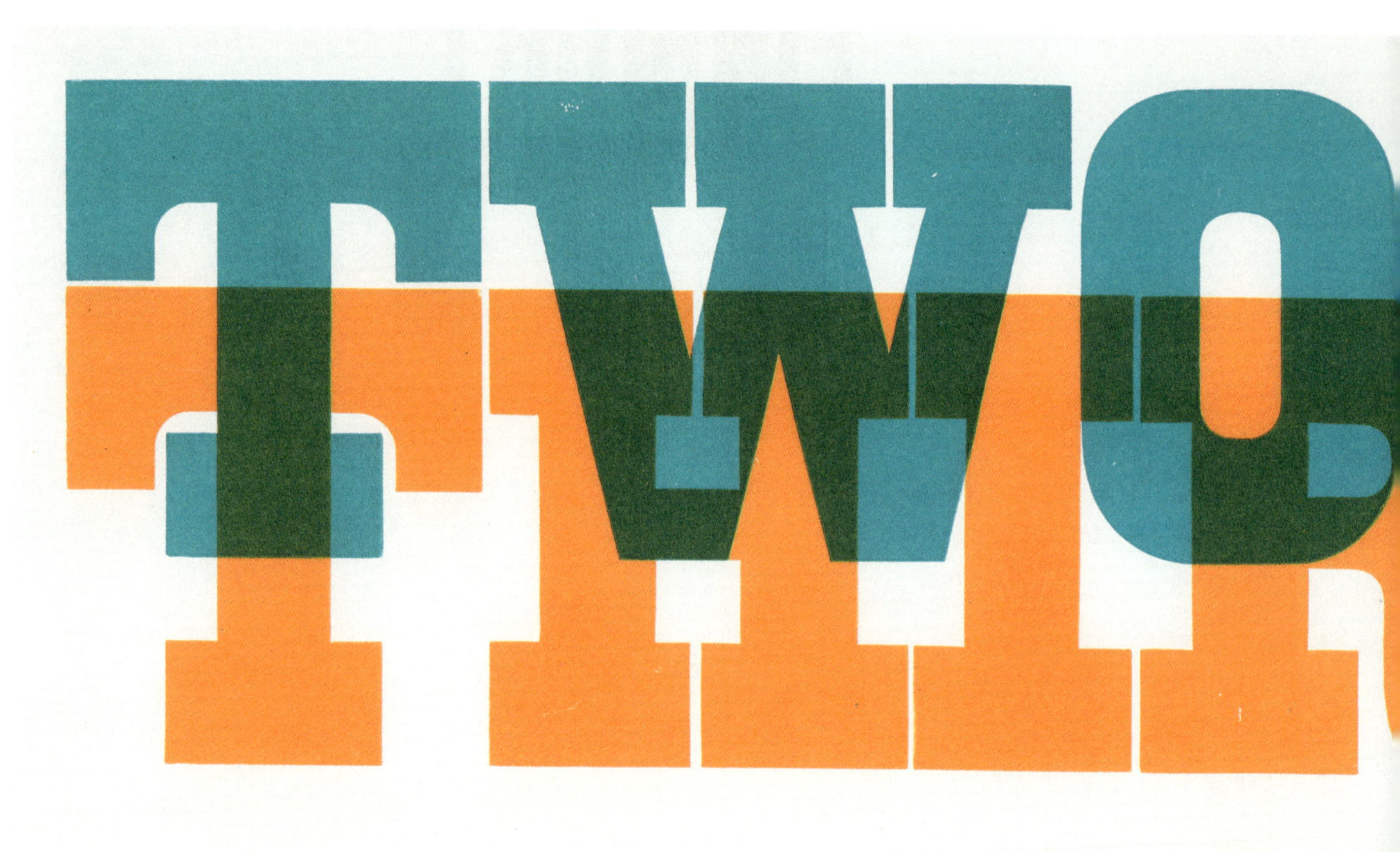
TWO

DS

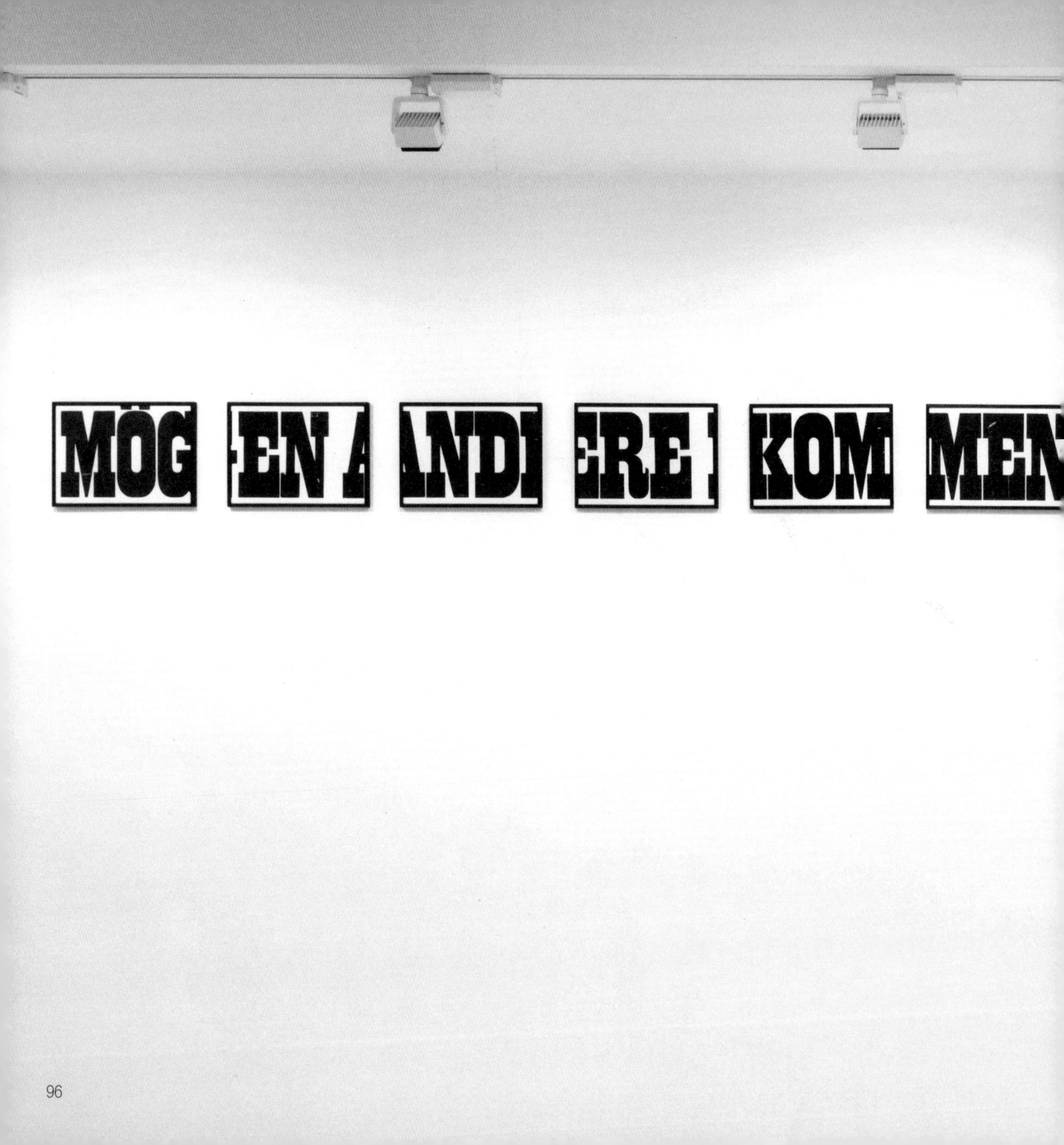

MÖG EN A NDE RE KOM MEN

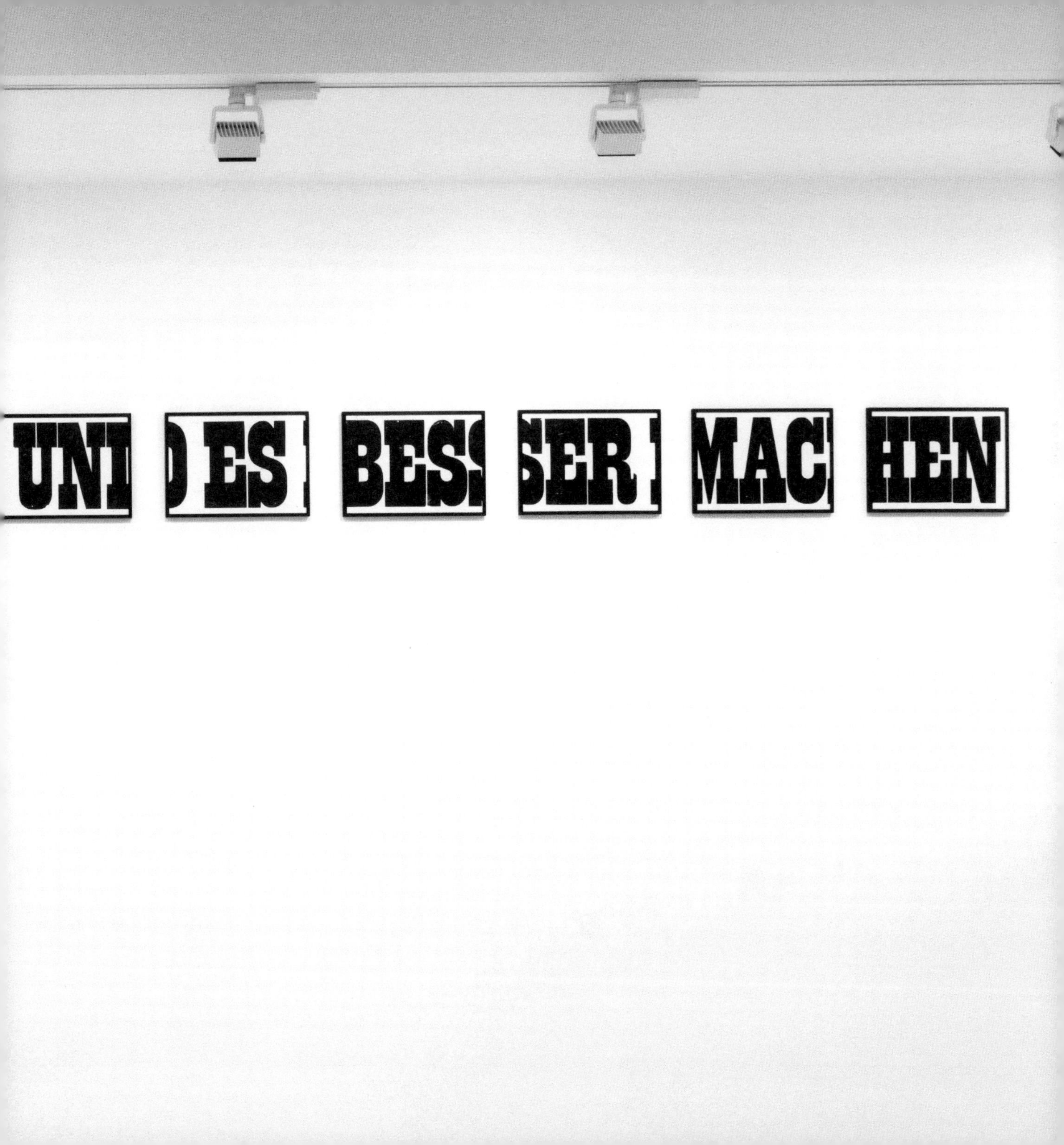

UND ES BESSER MACHEN

OTHER OPTIONS AVAILABLE

Tečka

za dobou kamennou.

All prints unique unless otherwise stated

2 AAABBDDEE, 2018
Letterpress from an incomplete set of type,
34 × 50 cm, wood type

5 Preface, 2016
Letterpress, 5 parts, 29.7 × 21 cm each

7 Honest Work (Honest), 2011
Letterpress from an incomplete set of type,
50 × 34 cm

9 Honest Work (Bottom), 2015
Letterpress from an incomplete set of type,
50 × 34 cm

11 Honest Work (Woods), 2011
Letterpress from an incomplete set of type,
50 × 34 cm

13 Honest Work (Signs), 2016
Letterpress from an incomplete set of type,
50 × 34 cm

15 Honest Work (Spirit), 2011
Letterpress from an incomplete set of type,
50 × 34 cm

17 Honest Work (Simple), 2012
Letterpress from an incomplete set of type,
50 × 34 cm

19 Honest Work (Worn), 2015
Letterpress from an incomplete set of type,
50 × 34 cm

21 Honest Work (As Red), 2011
Letterpress from an incomplete set of type,
50 × 34 cm

23 Honest Work (Violent), 2015
Letterpress from an incomplete set of type,
50 × 34 cm (edition 26 + 2)

24-25 Honest Work (Mutter), 2012
Letterpress from a sample of type,
50 × 34 cm, metal type

27 Honest Work (Unique), 2016
Letterpress from an incomplete set of type,
50 × 34 cm

28-29 Honest Work (Word / Words), 2013
Letterpress from an incomplete set of type,
2 parts, 50 × 34 cm each

31 Honest Work (Parole), 2013
Letterpress from an incomplete set of type,
50 × 34 cm

32 This. For Everyone., 2020
(Collaboration with Nick Thurston)
Letterpress, 21 × 59.4 cm (folded to
21 × 14.8 cm, blue version, unlimited
edition)

34-35 Three Gits, 2019
Letterpress from 3 incomplete sets of type,
37.5 × 51 cm, wood type

37 ABETCEDAIRE, 2012 (detail)
Letterpress, 34 × 50 cm (orange version)

39 Essential Elements, 2012
Letterpress, 34 × 50 cm (purple version)

40-41 Revolution of the Nineteenth
Century, 2012
Letterpress, 2 parts, 34 × 50 cm each
(red version)

43 One Hundred, 2012
Letterpress, 50 × 34 cm (green version)

45 New Work, 2012 (detail)
Letterpress, 112 × 76 cm

47 Honest Work (Received), 2016
Letterpress from an incomplete set of type,
50 × 34 cm (edition 35 + 2)

49 Honest Work (No Time), 2011
Letterpress from an incomplete set of type,
50 × 34 cm

50-53 Honest Work (Red Red), 2012
Letterpress from an incomplete set of type,
6 parts, 50 × 34 cm each

55 Human Condition, 2015
Letterpress from a single alphabet set,
34 × 50 cm (edition 15 + 2)

56-57 Honest Work (Question), 2017
Letterpress, 34 × 50 cm, wood type

59 Přikázání, 2018
Letterpress from a sample of type,
27 × 59 cm (edition 3 + 1)

60-61 Oops!, 2022
Letterpress from a mixed sample of type,
27 × 61.5 cm, plastic type

62/65 Beckett's Cage, 2019
Letterpress, 2 parts, 27 × 60 cm each
(edition 3 + 1)

66-67 The if in our life, 2023
Letterpress, 34 × 50 cm (print, edition 5 + 1)
and 22 × 46.5 cm (6-page foldout, unlimited
edition)

69 Still Life with Dust, 2017
Letterpress, dust on paper, 40 × 60 cm

71 In Progress, 2017
Letterpress, dust on paper, 40 × 60 cm

73 American Irish, 2012
Letterpress, 34 × 50 cm (brown version)

75 Nothing More, 2012
Letterpress, 34 × 50 cm (black version)

77 Faulty Puzzle, 2012
Letterpress, 50 × 34 cm

79 Philosophy of Composition, 2012 (detail)
Letterpress, 34 × 50 cm (blue version)

81 Do, 2012
Letterpress, 76 × 56 cm (edition 13 + 3)

82 Countdown, 2019
Letterpress, 27 × 60 cm, wood block,
certificate (series of 10)

85 Fifty, 2012
Letterpress, 34 × 50 cm

87 Twentysix, 2013
Letterpress, 34 × 50 cm

89 Honest Work (Five), 2012
Letterpress from an incomplete set of type,
50 × 34 cm (edition 3 + 1)

91 Honest Work (One), 2012
Letterpress from an incomplete set of type,
50 × 34 cm (edition 3 + 1)

93 Honest Work (Ein Wort), 2016
(Collaboration with Alex Lebus)
Letterpress from an incomplete set of type,
50 × 34 cm (edition 3 + 1)

95 Two Thirds, 2023
Letterpress, 27.5 × 63 cm (edition 3 + 2)

96 Probleme gelöst, 2016
Letterpress, 12 parts, 29.7 × 42 cm each

99 Options, 2023
Letterpress, 27 × 63.5 cm (edition 26 + 1)

100 Tečka, 2022
Letterpress, 27 × 60 cm (edition 5 + 1)

105 Fine, 2023
Letterpress, 34 × 59 cm

107 Je m'en étais bien douté, 2013 (detail)
Letterpress, 119 × 84 cm (edition 30 + 1)

FINE PRINT

Pavel Büchler: Variable Pieces

Edited by Pavel Büchler and Andrew Hunt
Designed by Pavel Büchler
Printed and bound by Page Bros, Norwich
Published by Slimvolume, 2023

Special thanks to annex14, Tanya Leighton,
and Tommy Simoens.

ISBN 978-1-910516-26-3

Distributed by
Cornerhouse Publications
HOME
2 Tony Wilson Place
Manchester M15 4FN
United Kingdom

Slimvolume
57c Davisville Road
London W12 9SH
United Kingdom

Slimvolume #27

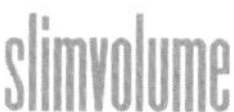

Front cover:
Honest Work (Variable), 2012 (detail)
Letterpress from an incomplete set of type,
50 × 34 cm

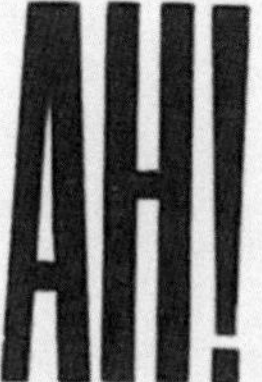